IMAM AL-GHAZALI

D1616242

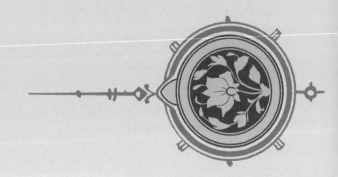

Imam
al-Ghazali

A CONCISE LIFE

Edoardo Albert

KUBE
PUBLISHING

To Harriet

First published in England by Kube Publishing Ltd,
Markfield Conference Centre, Ratby Lane, Markfield,
Leicestershire LE67 9SY, United Kingdom
Tel: +44 (0) 1530 249230
Fax: +44 (0) 1530 249656
Website: www.kubepublishing.com
Email: info@kubepublishing.com

Design, typesetting, maps, patterns, and illustrations
on pages 17, 22, 39, 49 and 59: Louis Mackay
Editor: Yosef Smyth

The author and publisher would like to thank the following for
their permission to reproduce pictures at short notice: Dean Askin
(Ruins of Tus 12); Navid Bahrami (Mausoleum of al-Ghazali 58); American
University of Beirut / Library Archives (Folios from al-*Tabr al-Masbuk
fi Nasihat al-Muluk wa al-Wuzara wa al-Wulat* 41).

Every effort has been made to trace and acknowledge ownership of copyright. The
publishers offer to rectify any omissions in future editions, following notification.

A Cataloguing-in-Publication Data record for this
Book is available from the British Library

ISBN 978-1-84774-030-4 paperback

Contents

Maps

Illustrations

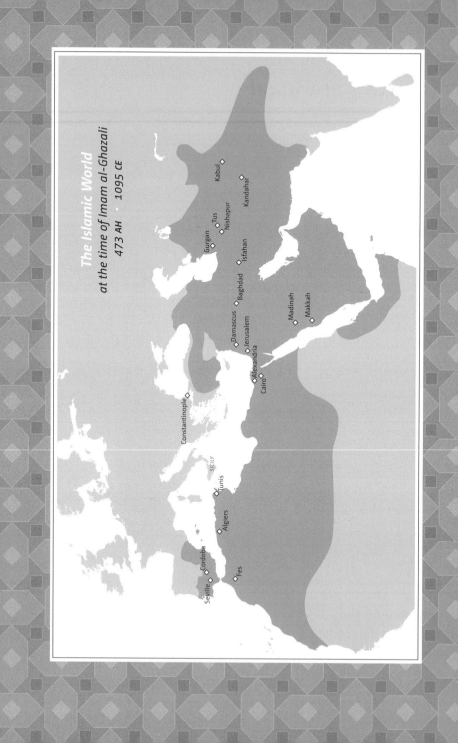

The Islamic World
at the time of Imam al-Ghazali
473 AH · 1095 CE

Kabul
Kandahar
Gurgan
Tus
Nishapur
Baghdad
Isfahan
Damascus
Jerusalem
Madinah
Makkah
Alexandria
Cairo
Constantinople
SICILY
Tunis
Algiers
Cordoba
Seville
Fes

Who was al-Ghazali?

Al-Ghazali was a Muslim saint, a scholar and, for a time,
a penniless wanderer seeking after God. He came from
a humble background and through intelligence and
determination became one of the most famous scholarly
authorities in the whole Islamic world. But then he gave
up all his power, prestige and money, and set off in search
of a deeper knowledge of God. Al-Ghazali looked for God
through philosophy, through Islamic law and even through
the claims of various alternative sects in Islam, but could
find Him in none of these places. In the end, al-Ghazali
found God through **mysticism**, a branch of religion that
seeks a spiritual experience of God. Following a new
mystical path, he also brought the living experience of
God to ordinary Muslims through his writings. For this
reason, and many others, he is recognised as the greatest
Muslim of his time and a timeless reviver of Islam. For
anyone seeking to understand Islam today, a knowledge
of al-Ghazali and his enduring influence on Muslims is
essential.

In a wider context, al-Ghazali lived at a time of
transition for the Muslim world, when it faced a set of
problems and challenges that have interesting parallels
with our own time. The breathless expansion of the early

centuries, when Muslim armies had conquered North Africa, the Middle East and started the long push into India, had ceased. Factions had arisen within the religion, with the Fatimids who ruled Egypt following a version of Islam that was at odds with the faith professed in Baghdad and Damascus. The ideas of the peoples into whose lands Islam's conquering armies had moved, most notably the Greeks, were percolating through sections of Muslim society, causing consternation, debate and confusion as to how they should be approached. It was a world where ideas mattered, and professing ideas that were at odds with powerful men could often have lethal repercussions.

This was the world into which al-Ghazali was born, and it was the world that his ideas were to transform. His writings were to a large measure responsible for defeating the heterodox ideas of the Fatimids, he defined the attitude that Muslims of subsequent centuries would take to Greek and other foreign philosophies, and the example of his life brought the lived experience of God within the ambit of ordinary Muslims.

The Islamic world of the time was very different from the West. Its cities, Baghdad, Damascus, Cairo, had comparatively huge populations. Power was concentrated in a small number of contending territories, each of which had ambitions to expand its control to take in the whole Muslim world. In contrast, in the West, the fall of Rome had produced an age of small kingdoms and fighting principalities – al-Ghazali was born just eight years before William the Conqueror led his small army across the

English Channel and defeated King Harold at the Battle of Hastings.

Al-Ghazali lived through the start of one of the key events in western medieval history: the Crusades. He was actually living in Jerusalem just a couple of years before the city was conquered by the Crusaders. Yet the fact that nowhere in his writings does he mention the Crusades indicates clearly the contemporary Muslim attitude to the invading westerners: for them, it was not particularly important. In fact, the Crusaders' success in establishing short-lived kingdoms in the Middle East was only possible because of fighting between Muslim states – once Saladin had established control of the region he destroyed the Crusader kingdoms in short order.

The flowering of Islamic civilisation that witnessed the life of al-Ghazali and the building of great mosques and centres of learning in Baghdad and elsewhere was brought to a shuddering, dreadful halt a century later, when the Mongols invaded and destroyed, well, almost everything. The Muslim world would recover from the trauma of those events, but it would take centuries. So this period when al-Ghazali lived and worked marked an apotheosis which, in some ways, could never be repeated.

The ruins of the Citadel of Tus, or Arg-e Tus, built during the
pre-Islamic Sassanid Empire and fortified under Muslim rule.

CHAPTER 1

Childhood

Al-Ghazali's full name was Abu Hamid Muhammad ibn Muhammad al-Ghazali. He was born in 1058 CE in what was at the time the city of Tus, which lies in present day Iran. However, there is no city there now because Tus was almost entirely destroyed during the Mongol invasion in 1220 CE.

Al-Ghazali's father, who was called Muhammad like his son, was a poor but devout man who made his living from spinning and selling wool. After work he often visited mosques, listening to the preaching of the **imams**, or sought out the company of **Sufis**.

Muhammad used to pray that he would have a son who was a great scholar and a preacher. But al-Ghazali's father did not live to see his prayer answered. He fell ill when al-Ghazali was very young, and knowing that he was dying, Muhammad asked a Sufi friend to oversee the upbringing of his two boys. He gave him all the money he had managed to save, on condition that it was used to pay for their education. For although he was uneducated himself, Muhammad wanted his two boys to receive as good an education as possible.

Unfortunately, we know almost nothing about al-Ghazali's mother, other than that she lived long enough

The Mongol invasions

In forty years the Mongol peoples, under the command of Genghis Khan, created the largest land empire the world has ever seen, stretching from China right across Asia and into the Middle East. Persia and Iraq were all but destroyed by them, with millions of people dying as a result of war and famine. 'There can be no doubt that even if for a thousand years to come no evil befalls the country, yet it will not be possible completely to repair the damage,' wrote one Persian historian. Yet, in time, the Mongol rulers converted to the religions of the lands they had conquered and set about repairing the damage their forefathers had done.

Genghis Khan in his tent by Rashid al-Din (1247–1318).

to see her son grow old. At the time in the Islamic world, it would have been thought unseemly to write about the female members of a family, and while al-Ghazali may have been unusual in writing an autobiography he did not break this other convention.

As a young student, al-Ghazali would have begun his studies by memorising the Qur'an and studying the *sunnah* of the Prophet Muhammad. Their guardian also told the two young boys stories of saints and holy men, as well as teaching them poetry. But al-Ghazali's father was a poor man and the money he had saved did not last long. When it ran out, the boys' guardian, who was poor himself, told them that the only way to continue their education was to go and become students at a *madrasah*.

A *madrasah* was a building often attached to a mosque where the main purpose was teaching. Here they would be given food as well as education. So that is what they did.

In his own words

❝ We sought learning for the sake of something other than God, but He would not allow it to be for anything but Himself. ❞

Al-Ghazali was from the start an avid reader and dedicated student. Later in his life, he warned young boys against chasing after a weary teacher walking home, firing fresh questions at him. It's possible that this warning was prompted by memories of how he hounded his teachers when he was young.

In al-Ghazali's day teachers taught lessons at their homes or at the nearest mosque. Here al-Ghazali sits cross-legged in front of a teacher, remonstrating with him. He and fellow students would have learned by heart the most important books. The best and brightest pupils were those who remembered most.

Interior of a *madrasah*.

EDUCATION IN AL-GHAZALI'S TIME

A generation or two before Europe's oldest universities (Bologna was founded in 1088 CE, Oxford in 1149 CE), most large cities in the Islamic world already boasted a *madrasah*. Whoever founded a *madrasah* would also fund an endowment to pay for general maintenance, professors' salaries and scholarships, ensuring that even poor students, alone and far from home, would have board and lodging.

Madrasahs were normally built with lecture rooms and libraries around a light and airy central courtyard. Most had both private libraries, solely for the use of students and professors, and public libraries that anyone could use. By the thirteenth century Baghdad had as many as thirty-six libraries.

The main study at most *madrasahs* was of Islamic law, but theology (religious philosophy), medicine, philosophy and all the sciences were also taught. Each teacher had fixed days, but there was no limit to how long a lecture could last, and some were very long indeed. Normally the class would copy down what the professor said as he spoke.

Starting at about the time al-Ghazali lived, there was a great flowering of Islamic thought and culture. Rulers valued learning and supported scholars, and scholars were held in high regard by the people. To find a teacher or to broaden their learning, it was common for scholars to travel great distances, and a famous lecturer would draw students from hundreds, even thousands, of miles away.

Travellers in a caravan, resting.

CHAPTER 2

The student

Al-Ghazali was an exceptionally bright and ambitious pupil. He read everything and always tried to get to the root of arguments. He must have been a difficult boy to teach, always piping up with questions and contradicting the teacher. The problem – and it was a problem that would come to haunt al-Ghazali – was that he was cleverer than many of his teachers, and he knew it.

Apart from the Qur'an, the young al-Ghazali learned Arabic grammar, theology, logic, Islamic law and **hadith**. Of these, the most important subject was Islamic law, or **shari'ah**. This was the body of laws – derived from the Qur'an, and the *hadith* and the personal example of the Prophet – that governed Muslim societies. Law was a good subject for an ambitious and able boy to study and al-Ghazali now needed to find somebody, somewhere, with the knowledge to teach him.

Studying a subject in depth in al-Ghazali's time meant finding the right teachers. So, in 1073 CE, al-Ghazali travelled to Gurgan, a town on the shores of the Caspian Sea some 500 kilometres (350 miles) from Tus to study law. He was only fifteen at the time but it was common for students to travel great distances to study under famous scholars.

The young student made careful notes of all he learned in Gurgan on Islamic law and set out back to Tus. However, on the way the caravan was attacked by bandits, who stole all the travellers had with them, including al-Ghazali's precious lecture notes. Although he was warned against doing so, al-Ghazali went after the robbers and begged them to give him back his notes. After all, they were of no value to anyone but him.

The bandit chief laughed and said, 'How can you lay claim to this knowledge when we have taken it from

Al-Ghazali pleads with bandits to return his precious notes, stolen on the return journey from Gurgan.

you? Now it belongs to us, not you. How can you call this knowledge when it is so easily taken away? Go, and think about this young scholar, and take your knowledge with you.' And then the leader of the robbers ordered his men to return the notes to al-Ghazali.

In his own words

" *The best advice I ever received was given to me by a robber.* "

Al-Ghazali took the robber's words as providential, and when he returned to Tus he set about memorising all his knowledge, so that it could never be taken away from him again. It took him three years.

Two brick constructions, known as Mehrva and Mehrabad or Shahmir, located 3 km south of Nishapur. The larger dome dates back to the eleventh century CE.

Chapter 3

The young sceptic

When he was twenty, al-Ghazali left Tus for the town of
Nishapur, which lay 70 kilometres (50 miles) to the west.
He went to Nizamiyyah Madrasah to study law and the
prevalent subject of philosophy under a famous teacher,
Imam al-Haramayn al-Juwayni (1028–1085 CE). Over
time the pupil proved cleverer than the teacher, and soon
al-Ghazali was lecturing his fellow pupils. He also began
writing his first book. When he showed it to Imam al-
Haramayn, his teacher is reported to have said, 'You have
buried me while I am still alive. Why did you not have the
patience to wait until I was dead? For your book has thrust
my writings out of sight.'

Al-Ghazali was on fire with the desire to know and
understand everything. But he soon realised that the
greatest obstacle between him and true knowledge was
accepting what parents and teachers said, unquestioningly.
Al-Ghazali would be bound by no such rules. He wanted
to question and challenge everything before believing it.

In his own words

**" He who does not doubt, does not investigate,
and he who does not investigate does not see, and he
who does not see remains in blindness and error. "**

But how could he be sure that *anything* was true? Al-Ghazali was certain of what he saw and felt and heard, but not much else. It was then that his search for truth really began.

In his own words

❝ **What I seek is knowledge of the true meaning of things. Of necessity, therefore, I must inquire into what the true meaning of knowledge is ... For the children of Christians always grow up embracing Christianity, and the children of Jews always grow up adhering to Judaism, and the children of Muslims always grow up following the religion of Islam.** ❞

This observation – that people follow the religion of their parents – made al-Ghazali wonder if we are all simply products of our environments, following helplessly in

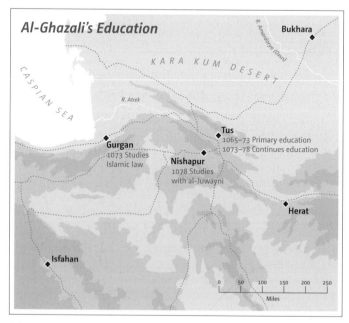

Al-Ghazali's Education

CASPIAN SEA

R. Amndarya (Oxus)

Bukhara

KARA KUM DESERT

R. Atrek

Tus
1065–73 Primary education
1073–78 Continues education

Gurgan
1073 Studies
Islamic law

Nishapur
1078 Studies
with al-Juwayni

Herat

Isfahan

0   50   100   150   200   250
Miles

LANGUAGE

Al-Ghazali was a Persian, and he both spoke and wrote in Persian. So the question arises, why did he learn Arabic and why are most of his works in this language? After all, Persian was (and is) a venerable language with an extraordinary literary heritage. But it was not the language of the Qur'an.

According to Muslim belief, the Qur'an is the uncreated word of God, the literal expression of his will, and those words are spoken in Arabic. Therefore, the Arabic language necessarily assumes a pre-eminent place within Islamic civilisation and in education. A Muslim must recite the requisite five daily prayers in Arabic, using the formula given in the Qur'an, whatever his or her own native language.

A consequence of this emphasis on Arabic was that it provided a *lingua franca*, uniting the disparate languages and cultures that were welded together under the banner of Islam. Thus a Persian scholar such as al-Ghazali could write in a language that would be understood by other Muslim scholars, from Spain in the west to India in the east. This common language allowed the transmission of Islamic ideas into widely disparate cultures, and the fertilisation of Islamic culture itself with ideas from those cultures.

Page of a Qur'an from Iran, eleventh/thirteenth century CE.

By al-Ghazali's time many new ideas about Islam were being developed. The huge expansion of the Islamic world had brought it into contact with many older philosophical traditions, most notably the Greek philosophers of antiquity. Muslim thinkers were faced with the task of adopting or rejecting these ideas for their faith. Different schools of philosophy developed in response to these ideas. Among them were the Mutazilites, a group of theologians who valued reason as the ultimate arbiter of truth and thus argued that reason held a higher place than revelation, and the Asharites, who denied that people can rely on reason for absolute truth and asserted that humans must rely on revelation from God.

the footsteps of the people who have taught or raised us. If that is the case, then there is no true knowledge of anything.

While al-Ghazali was searching for knowledge, he was also looking to advance in the world. After all, he came from a poor family and only by his own abilities could he improve his standing. The chance came after the death of his teacher, Imam al-Haramayn, in 1085 CE, when he was around twenty-seven years old. Luckily for al-Ghazali, a man from his home town, Tus, was now the most powerful man in the land. This man was Nizam al-Mulk, the **vizier** of the **sultans** of the Seljuq Dynasty.

Some time after the death of Imam al-Haramayn, al-Ghazali arrived at the court of Nizam al-Mulk. Already involved in political debate and familiar with the ruling class from his time at al-Nizamiyyah College this presented Ghazali with a new opportunity.

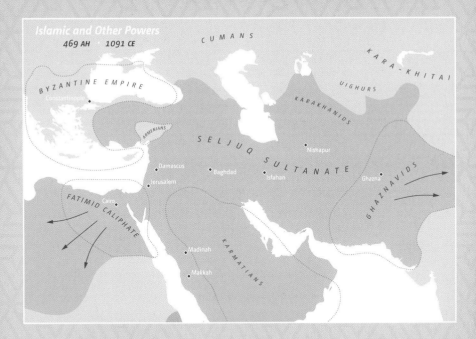

Islamic and Other Powers
469 AH · 1091 CE

CUMANS

BYZANTINE EMPIRE
Constantinople

KARA-KHITAI

UIGHURS

KARAKHANIDS

ARMENIANS

SELJUQ SULTANATE
Nishapur

Damascus
Baghdad
Isfahan
Ghazna

Jerusalem

GHAZNAVIDS

FATIMID CALIPHATE
Cairo

Madinah

KARMATIANS

Makkah

THE SELJUQS

During al-Ghazali's life, the Islamic world was split into several
different dominions, essentially ruled by families of warriors.
Egypt was ruled by the Fatimids, but another group, Turkish in
origin, had claimed control of Baghdad and thus controlled much
of the Islamic world. This group was called the Seljuqs.

On the death of Sultan Alp-Arslan in 1072 CE, his son
Malik-Shah ascended to the Seljuq throne. Malik was still young
and for many years real power lay in the hands of his vizier,
Nizam al-Mulk. A vizier, in effect the sultan's prime minister,
could wield great power, particularly if the sultan was young or
weak in character.

The Seljuqs ruled over a vast area, including the countries
today known as Iraq, Iran, Syria, Afghanistan, Turkmenistan,
Azerbaijan, Armenia, Georgia, much of Turkey, Oman, Jordan,
and part of Saudi Arabia, including the two Holy Cities of Makkah
and Madinah.

29

NIZAM AL-MULK (1018–1092 CE)

Nizam al-Mulk was born in Tus in 1018 and by 1063 he had risen to become vizier to the Seljuq sultans, serving first Alp-Arslan (1030–1072 CE) and then Malik-Shah (1055–1092 CE). As vizier, he represented the sultan throughout his lands. The Seljuq territory stretched from modern-day Turkey, through Iraq and Iran, and on into Central Asia – a huge area. Nizam al-Mulk was also a scholar and he did his best to support education by building many *madrasahs*. Indeed, it was said he instituted *madrasahs* in every city of Iraq and Khurasan.

His passion for knowledge also meant intelligent young scholars found a warm welcome in his entourage. Nizam al-Mulk even found time to write a manual on how to rule, called *The Book of Government*. In it he advises the sultan on how to run the domain, with chapters on politics, religion and the proper role of soldiers, police, spies and taxmen.

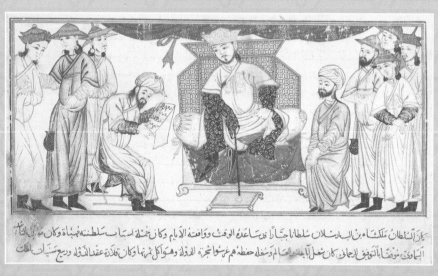

The Seljuq Sultan Malik-Shah in his court.
His vizier was Nizam al-Mulk.

Nizam al-Mulk's court was a travelling centre of administration, so the location of the meeting is unknown. Such was the organisation of the camp that in the space of a few hours an empty plain would become a city of tents, complete with a street of shops. But wherever Nizam was when al-Ghazali caught up with him, the young scholar received a warm welcome and was invited to join his court.

At the time al-Ghazali was already making a name for himself as a scholar, and good scholars were always honoured by the vizier. Even though he was only twenty-seven, al-Ghazali quickly took the lead among the group of travelling scholars that accompanied Nizam al-Mulk as his camp went from city to city. He spent six years in the vizier's court and took part in political debates and wrote books. During this period Nizam al-Mulk had the opportunity to assess the quality of the young man from Tus, and his judgment was clear. In 1091 CE, when al-Ghazali was thirty-four, Nizam al-Mulk approached him to ask if he wanted to be the principal of the al-Nizamiyyah College in Baghdad. This was similar to being made head of Oxford, Cambridge and Harvard universities combined, and al-Ghazali jumped at the chance. The penniless young boy from Tus was now the most one of the most important scholars in the Islamic world. Al-Ghazali had most definitely made it.

The establishment which would see al-Ghazali make his reputation, al-Nizamiyyah College in Baghdad, was founded by Nizam al-Mulk in 1065 CE. In a quarter of a

Baghdad besieged by the Mongols in 1258 CE, when
al-Nizamiyyah College was damaged.

century it had already become one of the most renowned centres of learning in the Islamic world. It was located on the eastern bank of the River Tigris, close to the wharf and market place. The college taught law, theology, philosophy and medicine, and the professors were free to teach whatever they wished. The teachers normally gave lectures, which the students would write down as the lecturer spoke.

The building was damaged during the Mongol conquest of Baghdad in 1258 CE and now no longer exists.

A preacher speaking in a mosque.

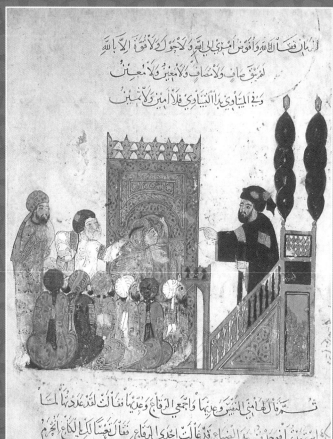

CHAPTER 4

Professor al-Ghazali

Once stationed as the chief teacher at the al-Nizamiyyah College, Ghazali quickly became known as one of the most eminent scholars in the Muslim world. Students came from throughout the Seljuq territories to hear him lecture and he was asked to give *fatwas* by people within their lands and rulers outside it. For example, the Muslim ruler of Spain, Yusuf bin Tashfin, sent messengers all the way to Baghdad to ask if it was permissible for him to depose the Muslim **amirs** who ruled the provinces of Spain largely independently.

The poor boy from Tus was now a wealthy, powerful and famous man and the number of people in his household – servants, attendants and students – was considerable.

Al-Ghazali was at the height of his powers, both intellectually and physically. But despite his success, he was a troubled man. The doubts that had plagued him since his youth, the uncertainty about whether he could know anything for certain, were rising to the surface of his mind again. He thought he could no longer even believe the evidence of his own senses, let alone anything else.

" *For nearly two months ... I was a sceptic in fact, if not in what I said. At length God Most High cured me of that sickness. My soul regained its health and equilibrium ... But the cure was not the result of thought or argument but on the contrary, it was the effect of a light which God Most High cast into my heart. And that light is the key to most knowledge.* "

In between all his other tasks, the young professor began to study even more deeply. He investigated the teachings of Muslim philosophers such as al-Farabi and Ibn Sina (who is sometimes called Avicenna after the Latin version of his name). These scholars had studied the philosophy of the ancient Greeks, in particular the ideas of Aristotle and Plato, and attempted to apply it to Islam.

Who was the caliph?

The caliph was the successor of the Prophet Muhammad as the leader and ruler of the Muslim community. However, by the time of al-Ghazali, the political power that the caliph once had was largely gone. The sultan and his vizier ruled.

For four years al-Ghazali studied their ideas, even writing a book called *The Aims of the Philosophers*, where he stated clearly what they thought. Al-Ghazali always insisted that it was first of all necessary to understand what someone was saying, and understand it thoroughly, before you could dispute it:

" *... one cannot recognize what is unsound in any of the sciences unless one has such a grasp of the furthest reaches of that science that you are the equal of those most learned in it. Then, and only then, will it be possible to see the errors it contains.* "

THE ARABIC PHILOSOPHERS (*FALASIFAH*)

The extraordinary expanse of territory and civilisations that Muslim armies conquered between the eighth and tenth centuries brought with them dilemmas as well as opportunities. The most pressing of these dilemmas in the time of al-Ghazali, was what to do about Greek philosophy. Many works by the great Greek philosophers of antiquity had been translated into Arabic and the ideas they espoused were gaining in influence, to the detriment of Islam in al-Ghazali's opinion. For instance, contemporary philosophers (called *falasifah* in Arabic) under the influence of Aristotle (384–322 BCE) challenged some key Muslim beliefs, such as the idea that the Qur'an was the revealed word of God.

A thirteenth century CE depiction of Aristotle teaching, by al-Mubashir.

Two of the most accomplished of these philosophers were al-Farabi (854–925/35 CE), who pioneered the application of human reason to the study of religion, arguing that it was superior to revelation, and Ibn Sina (980–1037 CE), who learnt Aristotle's philosophy from al-Farabi's work and continued to combine Greek philosophy with Islamic thought. Ibn Sina, who was also a doctor, mathematician, astronomer, poet, politician and traveller, was one of the most influential Muslims in history. He mastered all the fields of study of the time and is sometimes known as 'the man who knew everything'.

Al-Ghazali vehemently opposed the work and ideas of the *falasifah* and it was largely his arguments and books that prevented Greek philosophy from having much long-term influence in the Islamic world.

When al-Ghazali understood the philosophers, he wrote one of his greatest books, *The Inconsistency of the Philosophers,* to show their errors and in particular that man cannot understand God by his reason alone. Among other things that the philosophers taught contrary to the Qur'an, was the idea that the universe was eternal, and therefore God had not created it. This proclamation in al-Ghazali's time was not falsifiable and there was no obvious way to tell if the sun had been rising each morning forever, or whether there had been a first sunrise. Taking their lead from Aristotle, philosophers in Muslim lands such as Avicenna taught that the world was indeed eternal, co-existing with God and emanating eternally from him. Al-Ghazali set out to prove that this was wrong. The argument he used is simple:

1. whatever begins to exist has a cause

2. the universe began to exist

3. therefore the universe has a cause.

The key part of this argument is the second point. Al-Ghazali needed to demonstrate philosophically that the universe could not be infinitely old. For instance, he

Sunni and Shia

There are two main branches of Islam: Sunni and Shia. Today, Shia Muslims account for between 10 and 13 per cent of Muslims in the world, with most of them living in Iran, Iraq, Pakistan and India. Shia Muslims believe that the family and descendants of the Prophet Muhammad are the divinely appointed rulers of the Muslim community, and they revere a chain of leaders going back to the Prophet's son-in-law, Ali, and his two sons, Hasan and Husayn, the grandsons of Muhammad.

Ismailisim is regarded as a branch of Shia Islam.

knew that the earth's year is 365 days long, but one year for Jupiter takes twelve earth years. However, if both planets are infinitely old, then even though the earth has had twelve years for every one of Jupiter's, they are both the same age. On the back of paradoxes such as this, al-

The rock of Alamut, Iran. At the summit sits Alamut castle, Hassan-i-Sabbah's stronghold.

HASAN-I SABBAH (1056–1124 CE)

Hassan-i Sabbah was born in 1056 and converted to a sect of the Ismaili branch of Shia Islam after surviving an almost fatal illness.

Hasan-i Sabbah was determined to spread his version of Islam. First he needed a stronghold, and he found one in the castle at Alamut, which was set atop a huge rock and was near impregnable. Not having enough men to wage war, Hasan-i Sabbah trained his followers in stealth, spying and assassination. Political leaders whom he wished to intimidate might wake up in the morning to find a dagger lying on their pillow. The implication was that if they did not change their policies to something more in line with Hasan-i Sabbah's wishes, the next time the assassin would strike. Many historians believe that Nizam al-Mulk, a staunch supporter of Sunni Islam, was one of the men to die by the dagger of the assassins of Hasan-i Sabbah.

Ghazali concluded that the universe could not be infinitely old. And if the universe began to exist, then something or someone had to bring it into being. That someone was God.

By successfully refuting the arguments of the Arabic philosophers in the eyes of his contemporaries, al-Ghazali permanently weakened the influence of Greek philosophical thought in the Islamic world.

Al-Ghazali also inquired into the teachings of various Islamic sects, in particular a branch of the **Ismailis** called Batinites, who were led by the notorious Hassan-i Sabbah. The teachings of the Ismailis were particularly interesting to al-Ghazali because they taught that sure knowledge was available, through their leader, the imam. They believed that he was divinely guided, and thus all he said and taught must be true. However, al-Ghazali came to disagree, and he reserved some of the most severe rebukes in his books for them.

In his own words

" *Then we asked them about the lore they had learned from their infallible teacher, the Imam, and posed them some problems. These they did not even understand, let alone being able to solve them! Then, when they were unable to answer, they referred to the hidden imam and said, 'There is no alternative to making the journey to him.' The amazing thing is that they waste their life in seeking the authoritative teacher and in boasting of having found him, yet they have learned nothing at all from him! They are like a man smeared with*

The assassination of Nizam al-Mulk, from a Persian manuscript.

filth who wearies himself looking for water; then, when he finds it, he does not use it, but remains smeared with dirt! "

It is from the followers of Hassan-i Sabbah, the *Hashshasin*, that the word 'assassin' is derived, for they became known for their ability to kill anyone, no matter how powerful. It is likely that among their victims in al-Ghazali's time was his patron and benefactor, the vizier Nizam al-Mulk, who was killed in 1092 CE.

Later that same year, the sultan of the Seljuq dynasaty, Malik-Shah also died, leaving the political scene of the dynasty in turmoil. Baghdad was becoming a dangerous place for men associated with the old regime, and there were few closer to it than al-Ghazali. Yet, despite the political upheaval of the time and the threat from the 'assassins', al-Ghazali maintained his objections to the Ismaili sect's beliefs.

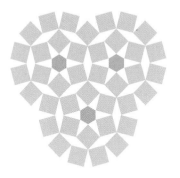

Folios from al-Ghazali's *Nasihat al-muluk*
(Book of Counsel for Kings), Mamluk Period.

CHAPTER 5

Crisis

The doubts and worries that had been plaguing al-Ghazali slowly came to a head in the years following the deaths of the vizier and the sultan. His quest for true knowledge had led him to study Islamic law, Greek philosophy and even the teachings of various religious sects, but he had found no certain answers there. Only in the mystical branch of Islam, **Sufism**, could al-Ghazali perceive some possibility of answering the questions that burned in his heart.

But there was a major problem with that attraction, particularly for a man who was a leading scholar of the Muslim world. Sufis were regarded with great suspicion by many Islamic jurists and theologians for their outspoken views. In rare cases, some, like al-Hallaj, had even been executed for blasphemy. For al-Ghazali to explore Sufism was to set aside reputation and status.

To understand why Sufis were regarded with suspicion by the wider Muslim world at the time, we need to go back to the extraordinary expansion of Muslim power and territory that occurred in the first two centuries of the religion. A faith that had been born in the desert

Sufism

Sufism is a movement within Islam which teaches that individual Muslims can have a direct and personal experience of God. Of course, you cannot just decide to do this, so you need a guide on your spiritual path, and that guide is the master or **shaykh** of a Sufi order. The **shaykh** can guide others to God because he himself has already drawn near to Him experientially.

among people who lived, out of necessity, the simplest of lives, became the bedrock of cultures and peoples that were immeasurably richer and more urban. Under the Umayyads (the caliphs who took control after the first four successors to the Prophet Muhammad), the capital of the Muslim world moved from Madinah, with its direct connection to the prophet, to Damascus. The Umayyads controlled a vast area and extraordinary wealth flowed to their capital. Such wealth and power brought great temptations in their wake, and many of the caliphs succumbed to those temptations. In reaction, there was a movement towards a return to the pure values of the Qur'an and a direct encounter with God. This movement became known as Sufism, and Sufis were soon in dispute with the legal authorities in Islam over various utterances and claims made by Sufis about their experiences of God.

A splendid group of Seljuq riders celebrating the end of Ramadan.

It was the direct encounter with God that was to prove the downfall of al-Hallaj. So taken up was he in the experience, that he reportedly proclaimed, 'I am the Truth!' Such was al-Hallaj's absorption in God that he ceased, for a while at least, to see himself as a separate creature. Such an assertion ran directly counter to the strict monotheism of Islam, as the fundamental profession of the religion is that there is no god but God. For al-Hallaj to claim he was the Truth – with a capital 'T' – was for him to say that he was God, and thus apparently negate the unity of God. This could not be allowed. And so, after being held in prison for eleven years, he was put to death in as gruesome a manner as the authorities could devise, being first crucified and then, while still alive, cut into pieces.

Al-Ghazali became convinced that it was only through the practice of Sufism that he could avoid 'falling into the Fire' and he resolved to mend his ways. But it was not to prove easy.

In his own words

" *I reflected on my intention in my public teaching, and I saw that it was not directed purely to God, but rather was instigated and motivated by the quest for fame and prestige ... I reflected on this for some time while I still had freedom of choice. One day I would firmly resolve to leave Baghdad and change my life, and another day I would revoke my resolution. I would put one foot forward and the other backward. In the morning I would have a sincere decision to seek the things of the afterlife; but by evening the hosts of passion would assail it and render it lukewarm ... I would make an irrevocable decision to run off and escape.*

Then Satan would return to the attack and say, 'This is a passing state: beware of yielding to it! For it will quickly vanish. Once you have given up your present renown and splendid position, your soul might again look longingly at all that but it would not be easy to return to it!' "

The conflict raged in his mind and heart for some six months. Then al-Ghazali, one of the most famous scholars in the Islamic world, the man to whom students travelled from all over the world, lost the power of speech. He was suffering a complete breakdown.

He tried to speak, and to carry on with his lectures, but he could not force the words from his mouth. All the worldly ambitions he had struggled to achieve – fame, position, wealth – were slipping from his grasp. Desolate and despairing, al-Ghazali could hardly eat or drink and his health began to fail. The sultan – the successor to Malik-Shah – even sent his own doctors to try and cure al-Ghazali, but they could do nothing.

In his own words

" Then, when I saw my powerlessness, and when my capacity to make a choice had completely collapsed, I had recourse to God and I was answered by Him. He made it easy for my heart to turn away from fame and fortune, family, children, and friends. I announced that I had resolved to leave for Makkah, all the while planning to secretly travel to Syria. This I did as a precaution, lest the caliph and my friends might learn that I wanted to settle in Damascus. Therefore I made use of clever stratagems about leaving Baghdad, while firmly resolved never to return to it. I was much talked about by the religious leaders, since none of them believed that my leaving had a religious motive. For they thought my post was the highest honour in our religion. "

Before leaving Baghdad, al-Ghazali gave up his teaching post to his brother, Ahmad, and gave away most of his money, keeping back only enough to ensure the education and livelihood of his children. Then he left, setting out upon the road to Damascus in the clothes of a poor man. He did not intend to come back.

Dome of the Rock, Jeruslem, founded in 691 CE
by the Umayyad Caliph Abd al-Malik.

CHAPTER 6

A new life

It was nearly five hundred miles from Baghdad to
Damascus, and al-Ghazali probably covered much of
that distance on foot. It was, however, commonplace for
scholars to travel in the Islamic world, seeking knowledge
and experience from their journey. For instance, a
contemporary of al-Ghazali named al-Tabrizi, who was
also a professor at the al-Nizamiyyah College,

> … had no money to hire a horse, so he put his book into a
> sack and began to walk the long journey from Persia to Syria.
> The sweat on his back oozed through the material of his sack
> and stained the manuscript, which was long preserved and
> shown to visitors in one of the libraries of Baghdad.

Al-Ghazali was trying to leave his fame behind, so he
arrived in Damascus quietly, going to the Umayyad
Mosque and taking care to tell no one that he was really
the most renowned scholar in the Islamic world.

In his own words

**" I lived in Damascus for nearly two years. My only
occupation was seclusion and solitude and spiritual
exercise and combat with a view to devoting myself to
the purification of my soul and the cultivation of virtues
and cleansing my heart for the remembrance of God**

Most High, in the way I had learned from the writings of the Sufis. I used to pray in seclusion for a time in the mosque, climbing its minaret for the whole day and shutting myself in. "

But al-Ghazali did not spend all his time in prayer while in Damascus, for it was during this period – after leaving Baghdad – that he wrote probably his most important book, *The Revival of the Religious Sciences.*

Al-Ghazali had ascended to the heights of the Islamic world in his previous career as a scholar, but found that there was something lacking in how the religion was presented to Muslims of his time, for he himself sought a deeper knowledge and could not find it in most of the avenues open to him. Sufism provided a way into the heart of Islam for him, but he also wanted to revive the religion for all Muslims. To do so he wrote this vast book, of some one thousand pages, bringing out much of the hidden depths of ordinary Islamic worship, and then leading the reader by the hand on a journey towards God, showing how He might be reached and some of the traps and pitfalls along the way.

The book is divided into four sections. The first part deals with the practices and requirements placed upon Muslims by their faith such as prayer, fasting, ritual purity, and pilgrimage. The second part of the *Revival* looks at the laws governing the interactions between an individual and society, particularly in relation to marriage, friendship and work. The third part seeks to identify those acts and behaviours that will lead to hell – al-Ghazali is here acting

THE UMAYYAD MOSQUE

The Umayyad mosque in Damascus where al-Ghazali spent most of his time is one of the great buildings of the Islamic world, with space for 20,000 people to pray. It was built between 706 and 715 CE, making it one of the oldest mosques in the world, on the site of a Christian church dedicated to John the Baptist. The Arab conquerors of Syria required the local Christian population to sell the church so that the mosque could be built and it still contains the head of John the Baptist, who is revered as a prophet under the name of Yahya by Muslims. One of the minarets of the mosque is called Isa (Jesus), and it was in this tower that al-Ghazali secluded himself.

An early photograph of the al-Aqsa Mosque in Jerusalem.

THE HOLY CITY OF JERUSALEM

Jerusalem could lay claim to being the most sacred city in the world, since it is a key holy site for Jews, Christians and Muslims. For Muslims it is sacred not only with respect to the Jewish prophets and kings who are honoured in the Qur'an, such as Solomon and David, but for Jesus, who also holds a high place within Islam and then, finally, for Muhammad too. Muslims believe that the Prophet was taken by the angel Gabriel from Jerusalem up into heaven from here. The al-Aqsa Mosque, which is built atop the site of the old Jewish temple that was destroyed by the Romans in 70 CE, commemorates and marks the site of the Prophet's ascent. It is regarded as the third most holy site in Islam, after Makkah and Madinah.

as a guide, warning his readers of where the dangers in this life occur – and advises how to avoid them. And the fourth part of the *Revival* reverses the section before, going into the virtues that a Muslim should seek to develop in order to achieve salvation on his or her death.

The key thought running through *The Revival of the Religious Sciences* is the same realisation that changed al-Ghazali's life in the everyday world: even the longest life is but a fleeting instant when compared to eternity, yet the actions made during those few short years determine what happens to us in eternity. In the light of this conviction, it is no surprise that al-Ghazali rails against wordly success and fortune. After all, what profit is it to a man to gain the whole world and lose his own soul? From reading the Sufis, al-Ghazali had come to believe that what counted in God's eyes was not our theological convictions but what we *did* in this life. Seeing hell as a real possibility if he continued on his worldly path, al-Ghazali abandoned his career and turned to a life of prayer. *The Revival of the Religious Sciences* was intended to help other people take the path to heaven and avoid the road to hell.

For al-Ghazali, Muslims should strive to follow the example of the Prophet in all things. This is a normal part of Muslim teaching but al-Ghazali goes into much greater psychological detail as to how to go about doing this. After all, people have had the experience of resolving to do something and failed in their resolutions. To overcome this perennial human failing, al-Ghazali said we must learn to discipline the soul. This is because, right from birth, a human being is incomplete and inclined towards doing the wrong thing. This tendency is all too easily exacerbated by bad influences from other people and society in general. Therefore we need to make great efforts over a long period of time, patiently trying again after each failure, to develop virtuous character traits. We can be helped in this by our education, by the precepts of religion, by what we read and, hopefully, through the general moral climate in which we live. Although al-Ghazali advocated disciplining the soul, he did not say people should give up those potentially dangerous but nonetheless powerful emotions such as anger and sexual desire. These are part of human nature, and therefore natural; they cannot be obliterated but must instead be controlled using one's mind. This, not surprisingly, can be a long process and even for the best person controlling these volcanic parts of the psyche requires constant training. In fact, al-Ghazali likens training the soul to training a young horse: it needs to be broken, trained and nurtured.

Being all too aware, from his own experience, of the temptations of worldly power and prestige, al-Ghazali suggested that the religious law under which Muslims lived should try to create a culture and environment conducive to people's wellbeing and their living virtuously. Al-Ghazali based this idea on the belief that God's law, the *shari'ah*, was intended to help people in this world and the next. That is, by aiding people to live good lives in this world God's law ensured heavenly bliss in the next world. But what do people require in order to live good lives in this world? Al-Ghazali said there were five key elements to the good life: religion, life, intellect, children and homes. Therefore, any law or custom that helped these 'five necessities' should be pursued, while whatever acted against them should be avoided or overturned. So any religious judge should, in his rulings, aim to look after the 'five necessities'.

Al-Ghazali's fame was too great for him to remain unknown in Damascus. One day he overheard a professor in one of the colleges of Damascus begin a lecture with the words, 'Al-Ghazali said ...' At this he felt the swelling of his old pride in his intellect. Not wanting to run the risk of his old failing returning to master him, al-Ghazali decided to leave the city and take up again the life of a wandering pilgrim. He left Damascus and although historians are not certain about the order of his travels, most think that he travelled first to Jerusalem. Al-Ghazali himself says that he visited the Dome of the Rock in Jerusalem and stayed there for some time locked away in prayer.

Al-Ghazali does not tell us any more about how he

Al-Ghazali's
pen case.

spent his time in Jerusalem, but we can be certain that much, if not most, of his time was devoted to prayer. In his book, *The Revival of the Religious Sciences*, he writes on how a Muslim can draw closer to God.

In his own words

" *From many verses of the Qur'an it appears that the only way of becoming united with God is constantly to seek Him. This is the point of a prayer called the* **wird***, which the believer can say at all times of day and night. There are seven* wirds *to say during the day... and five* wirds *during the night.* "

These prayers were in addition to the five daily prayers obligatory to all Muslims, and al-Ghazali also recommended the practice of *dhikr*, the remembrance of God. With so much of his life devoted to prayer, it is a wonder that al-Ghazali found time to eat and sleep, let alone write, but he did.

What al-Ghazali was doing here was combining a form of worship that was new in his life, the practical spirituality of Sufism, with the more traditional practices of theoretical knowledge, study, and ritual prayer that had filled his life up until now. This new path provided him with a contentment and a certainty that had been missing in Baghdad. Furthermore, his new approach allowed for the reconciliation of revelation and reason, allowing them both a place in Islamic philosophy.

From Jerusalem al-Ghazali went to Hebron to visit the tomb of Abraham, the common father of the world's three monotheistic religions. From Hebron, al-Ghazali finally made the **hajj** which he had said he was setting out upon when he first fled Baghdad. Although he does not mention travel companions directly in his books, it is certain that he would have set out on most of these long journeys with other travellers. After all, it was al-Ghazali who once said, 'First the companion, then the road.'

Mausoleum of
al-Ghazali, Tus.

CHAPTER 7

Going back to his roots

It is hard to tell exactly what al-Ghazali did after visiting Makkah. Abd al-Ghafir, a friend of al-Ghazali, says that he returned to Syria, went a second time to Makkah, and then spent some ten years wandering from shrine to shrine. But we do know, and this from al-Ghazali himself, that at some point he did what he had sworn he would never do: he returned to Baghdad.

Al-Ghazali tells us that he returned to the city in answer to 'certain concerns and the appeals of my children'. However, he returned a very different man. No longer was he the proud and ambitious scholar, now he had become a wandering traveller, careless of anything save drawing nearer to God.

In his own words

" *There I also chose seclusion out of a desire for solitude and the purification of my heart for the remembrance of God. But current events and important family matters and gaining the necessities of daily life had their effect and disturbed my solitude, so that the pure state of spiritual ecstasy occurred only intermittently. But I did not cease to seek after it. Obstacles would keep me away from it, but I would return to it.* **"**

The Sacred Mosque at Makkah. Shown on a Turkish tile, seventeenth century CE

Among those obstacles was the fact that al-Ghazali could not remain anonymous in Baghdad for long. Soon people started to request he preach and teach, and in the end he did so. However, his brother, Ahmad, himself a Sufi, went to see al-Ghazali, and recited this verse:

> You have sought to guide others and have not guided yourself,
> Men listen to your preaching but you do not listen to theirs,
> O whetstone, how long will you sharpen iron,
> And yet not receive a cutting edge yourself?

Al-Ghazali was already becoming dissatisfied with himself as a preacher. He wrote in a letter, 'I do not think myself worthy to preach.' In addition to this sense of unworthiness, he was growing homesick.

In his own words

" *He has made their native lands dear unto men,*
Places wherein their hearts long to be
When men remember their homes, they are mindful
Of childish days there and they yearn for return. **"**

A student at one of al-Ghazali's lectures heard him recite the verse above and, having done so, al-Ghazali wept and his listeners wept too. With his brother telling him to go and his own homesickness, al-Ghazali decided to leave Baghdad, this time for good. With his wife and children he returned to his native town of Tus and settled down there, leading a life of seclusion, study and prayer. Although he had withdrawn from society, al-Ghazali was still happy to help anyone who came to him seeking spiritual guidance.

A teacher and his students in the library at Basra, Iraq.

But unfortunately for his contented spiritual state, one of the men who sought him was Fakhr al-Mulk, the successor as vizier to the great Nizam al-Mulk.

The new vizier had heard that al-Ghazali the scholar, who was now as well known for his holiness as his intelligence, lived in little Tus, and on his travels around the Seljuq territories he called on al-Ghazali to ask his blessings and hear his teaching. But having met al-Ghazali, the vizier decided that such a man was far too precious to be left in seclusion in a small town far away from anywhere important. So Fakhr al-Mulk asked al-Ghazali to come out of retirement and resume public teaching, although this time not in Baghdad but the far nearer Nishapur, where al-Ghazali had studied as a child.

Viziers are hard men to refuse when they insist, but al-Ghazali also came to believe that it was God's will that he come out of retirement to fight against the decay of faith among Muslims. So in 1106–1107 CE, al-Ghazali started lecturing at the college in Nishapur. He was a very different man now from the young and ambitious, not to say arrogant, scholar he had once been.

An old friend, Abd al-Ghafir, who had known al-

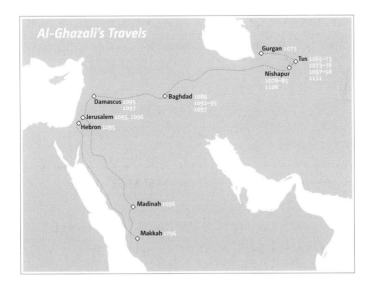

Ghazali before he renounced the world and took up prayer and contemplation, was amazed by the change. In fact, he suspected that al-Ghazali was simply putting on an act of saintliness. After investigation he decided that the man was not acting. Such was the transformation that Abd al-Ghafir concluded that it was as if al-Ghazali had regained his sanity after a long attack of madness:

> However much he met of contradiction and attack and slander, it made no impression on him, and he did not trouble to answer his assailants. I visited him many times and he was the opposite of what he had been before and purified from those faults. Before he had often spoken roughly to people and looked upon them contemptuously if they lacked his own ease of word and thought and expression, or they were not equal to his own rank and position. I realised after investigation that the man had recovered after being mad.

One of al-Ghazali's key achievements was the rapprochement between Islamic jurisprudence and Sufism. He did this, more than anything, by living the reconciliation of these two methods in his own life: a leading jurist in the Muslim world became a Sufi and found in Sufism the direct experience of God that his soul and intellect craved, yet afterwards he continued to give legal judgments and accept absolutely the necessity of Islamic law for the right ordering of society and the pursuit of an individual's path to God.

Fakhr al-Mulk followed his predecessor, Nizam al-Mulk, in a less pleasant way: he was assassinated. No longer under orders from the government, al-Ghazali retired one last time from public life and returned to Tus. The strains and trials of his many years of travel had worn him down and al-Ghazali died in Tus on Monday, 18 December 1111 CE (14 Jumada II 505AH). He was fifty-three years old.

Al-Ghazali's brother, Ahmad, who was there at the end, said this about the way he met his death:

> On Monday, at dawn, my brother performed the ablution and prayed. Then he said, 'Bring me my grave clothes,' and he took them and kissed them and laid them on his eyes and said, 'Most gladly do I enter into the presence of the King.' And he stretched out his feet towards Makkah, and was taken to the good will of God Most High.

Folio from al-Ghazali's *Alchemy of Happiness*.

CHAPTER 8

What was al-Ghazali like?

What was al-Ghazali like as an individual? There are many clues in what we have learned of his life so far, but there is more that can be guessed at from his writings.

His intelligence is the dominating characteristic of his early life. It certainly did not diminish as he grew older, but other traits came to prominence in his personality. For such a solitary man, al-Ghazali was surprisingly sociable. He said that it is good to eat in company as that means there will be friendly conversation during meals. He was almost certainly a keen chess player, for he tells us that a master of the game cannot stop himself instructing others, and that the master will sacrifice knight and castle without hesitation if it means winning the game.

Friendship was important to al-Ghazali, for he tells us, 'The believer both gives and receives friendship and there is no good in anyone who does neither.' But for a friendship to succeed, al-Ghazali believed five things were necessary.

1. Intelligence. Al-Ghazali thought no good could come from hanging around with fools, going so far as to say that an intelligent enemy was better than a stupid friend.

2. A good character, that is someone who can control himself and not let anger or lust overpower him.

3. Good morals. You should not seek the friendship of people who do evil and persist in it.

4. Freedom from greed. A greedy friend is, according to al-Ghazali, like poison to the soul.

5. Sincerity. A friend must be trustworthy, for someone who cannot be trusted is 'like a mirage which makes what is distant seem near to you and what is near seem far away'.

Al-Ghazali was fond of animals, even speaking well of dogs, an animal not often liked by Muslims. But cats were particular favourites and he tells a story of how a particular Sufi learned to sit completely still and quiet while praying, 'I learned it from a cat we had. When she was seeking her prey she used to sit by the mouse hole and never stir a hair.' He insisted particularly that people should not ill-treat the animals that worked for them, such as camels, horses and donkeys.

Al-Ghazali's brother, Ahmad, survived him by fifteen years but of his sisters and mother we know very little, it not being customary at the time to write about the women of a family. We do know, however, that the mother of these two remarkable boys lived long enough to go with them to Baghdad and see them both established.

Al-Ghazali was married, but there is no record of his wife's name. However, it seems to have been a happy marriage, for he writes that the companionship and cheer of a wife dispels sadness and brings joy to the heart. In fact, he says a good wife is highly important for a man's religious life, and presumably the opposite holds true, although he does not state it.

Al-Ghazali and his wife had three daughters and at least one son, but the boy seems to have died when he was young, since only the daughters were alive when al-Ghazali himself passed on. However, since we know that one of his daughters, Sitt al-Nisa, had a son called Ubayd, then it is likely that al-Ghazali became, and enjoyed being, a grandfather in his later years.

In conclusion, let us look at why al-Ghazali is such an important figure in the history of Islam. On the intellectual level, he decisively defeated the philosophers who wanted to import Greek thought into Islam. But what he did for the place of mysticism and Sufism within Islam is even more important. By his teaching and example, he brought their spiritual characteristics from being a rather suspect fringe activity into a place near the heart of the religion. It was now acceptable to be a Sufi and seek after an experience of God's presence. As one of al-Ghazali's biographers says:

Chess players, from a Persian manuscript, *A Treatise on Chess*. Al-Ghazali's writings suggest that he was a keen chess-player.

He was convinced that true religion must always be a matter of personal experience, and it was because his own teaching was so plainly the result of his own spiritual experience and a reflection of his own inner life, that his leadership was acknowledged and men counted him as one of the greatest ... friends of God.

In a wider context, al-Ghazali was important as one of the writers who transmitted knowledge of Greek thought, particularly Aristotle, to Europe. This came about largely through the efforts of translators in Spain, which was then under Muslim rule but had a large Jewish and Christian population. Al-Ghazali's works were translated into Castilian by Avendeath (who also appears as Johannes Hispanus, and John of Seville), who lived in Toledo, and Dominic Gundisalvus. From the Castilian text, they were then translated into Latin, and became part of the vibrant intellectual universe that produced the greatest and most profound of the medieval Jewish thinkers, Maimonides (1135–1204).

In one of those strange ironies of history, the work of al-Ghazali that was to have the most lasting and profound impact on people outside the Muslim world was his *The Aims of the Philosophers*, in which he sought to give a clear and fair account of Aristotle's teaching. This book was translated into Latin and became very influential among medieval Christian theologians and philosophers; St Thomas Aquinas (1225–1274), the greatest theologian of his time, refers to it frequently. The irony was that the Europeans thought that al-Ghazali accepted the ideas he set out in *The Aims of the Philosophers* when, of course, he did not. This does, however, quite accurately reveal the different ways in which the Muslim and Christian worlds reacted to and appropriated Greek thought into their own world views: the Muslim approach was to analyse what was compatible in Greek thought with Islam and reject what was not, whereas Christian scholars, in the end, sought to reconcile and synthesise the different approaches.

Al-Ghazali's brother, Ahmad, wrote a poem which was found beside him at his death. It could as well have been written by al-Ghazali himself.

> Say to my friends, when they look upon me, dead,
> Weeping for me and mourning me in sorrow
> Do not believe that this corpse you see is myself.
> In the name of God, I tell you, it is not I,
> I am a spirit, and this is naught but flesh
> It was my abode and my garment for a time...
> I am a bird, and this body was my cage...
> Praise be to God, Who hath now set me free...
> Now, with no veil between, I see God face to face.
> I look upon the Tablet and therein I read
> Whatever was and is and all that is to be...
> What I am now, even so shall you be,
> For I know that you are like unto me...
> I give you now a message of good cheer
> May God's peace and joy be yours evermore.

Timeline

1058 CE	Al-Ghazali born in Tus (today in Iran).
1073	Al-Ghazali travels 500 kilometres (350 miles) to Gurgan to study law.
1078	Al-Ghazali goes to Nizamiyyah Madrasah in Nishapur to study law and philosophy.
1085	Al-Ghazali arrives at the court of Nizam al-Mulk.
1091	Al-Ghazali becomes the principal at the al-Nizamiyyah College in Baghdad.
1092	Nizam al-Mulk is assassinated.
1092	Malik-Shah, sultan of the Seljuq Dynasty, dies.
1095	Al-Ghazali breaks down and becomes incapable of speech.
1095	Al-Ghazali leaves Baghdad.
1095	Al-Ghazali arrives in Damascus. He starts writing *The Revival of the Religious Sciences*.

1096	Al-Ghazali visits Jerusalem and lives there for a number of months.
1096	Al-Ghazali completes the *hajj*, the pilgrimage to Makkah.
1096	Al-Ghazali finishes *The Revival of the Religious Sciences*.
1096–1106	Al-Ghazali wanders from town to town and shrine to shrine.
1106	Starts teaching at the Nizamiyyah Madrasah in Nishapur.
1111	Al-Ghazali dies in Tus, his home town.

Glossary

Amir	a governor or ruler of a territory, usually under the overlordship of a sultan.
Dhikr	the constant remembrance of God by repeating His name or a formula containing His name, such as the Muslim testimony of faith: there is no god but God.
Fatwa	nonbinding legal opinion of an Islamic scholar.
Hadith	the sayings and actions of the Prophet Muhammad.
Hajj	the pilgrimage to Makkah. This is one of the Five Pillars of Islam and all Muslims should attempt to carry it out once in their lifetime.
Imam	a Muslim leader; commonly associated with the chief of a community, or the religious leader of a mosque.
Madrasah	A school where people go to learn about the religion of Islam.
Mysticism	that branch of religion that seeks after a direct and personal knowledge and experience of God.

Shari'ah	the divine law as found in the Qur'an and the words and actions of the Prophet Muhammad (*Sunnah*).
Sufi	a Muslim seeking after direct experience of God. Sufis follow a particular spiritual master, or sheikh.
Sufism	the mystical branch of Islam.
Sultan	ruler.
Sunnah	the traditional portion of Muslim law based on Muhammad's words or acts.
Vizier	the chief minister of the ruling sultan. Viziers could sometimes be more powerful than the sultans in whose name they ruled.
Wird	a passage from the Qur'an, or some other act of worship, which a Sufi repeats regularly.

Bibliography

Griffel, Frank (2009). *Al-Ghazali's Philosophical Theology.* Oxford University Press.

MacDonald, Duncan B. (2010). *The Life of al-Ghazzali, with Especial Reference to His Religious Experiences and Opinions.* Gorgias Press.

McCarthy, R. J. (1980). *Deliverance from Error: an Annotated Translation of al-Munqidh min al Dalal and other relevant works of Al-Ghazali.* Fons Vitae.

Watt, William M. (1982). *The Faith and Practice of Al-Ghazali.* Kazi Publications.

Smith, Margaret (1983). *Al-Ghazali the Mystic: a study of the life and personality of Abu Hamid Muhammad al-Tusi al-Ghazali, together with an account of his mystical teaching and an estimate of his place in the history of Islamic mysticism.* Hijra International Publishers.

Zwemer, Samuel M. (1920). *A Moslem Seeker after God: showing Islam at its best in the life and teaching of Al-Ghazali mystic and theologian of the eleventh century.* Fleming H. Revell Company.

Further reading

The best place to learn more about Al-Ghazali is of course his own works. These are now widely available in English translations:

Al-Ghazali (2005). *Letter to a Disciple*. Islamic Texts Society.

Al-Ghazali (1995). *Disciplining the Soul/Breaking the Two Desires*. Islamic Texts Society.

Since so much of al-Ghazali's work dealt with Greek philosophy, and the dialogue with these seminal thinkers has continued on into the modern day, then anyone seeking to broaden their knowledge should read Plato and Aristotle, or books about them:

Plato (2011). *The Last Days of Socrates*. Penguin.

Adler, Mortimer J. (1992). *Aristotle for Everybody: Difficult Thought Made Easy*. Collier Paperbacks.

Aristotle (2004). T*he Nicomachean Ethics*. Penguin.

Index

The author

Edoardo Albert is a London-based writer of Italian and
Sri Lankan extraction. He specialises in religion, travel and
archaeology, and gets up early in the morning (5am!) to
write stories. To find out more about his work, visit
www.edoardoalbert.com